HARISMITA VAIDESWARAN

ULTIMATE INDIAN

CRICKET

CHAMPIONS

SHUBMAN GILL

juggernaut

JUGGERNAUT BOOKS
C-I-128, First Floor, Sangam Vihar, Near Holi Chowk,
New Delhi 110080, India

First published by Juggernaut Books 2025

10 9 8 7 6 5 4 3 2 1

P-ISBN: 9789353453183
E-ISBN: 9789353452667

Typeset in Futura Std by R. Ajith Kumar, Noida

Printed at Thomson Press India Ltd

For Cakrin and Delphi

Love you, brother mine,
thanks for all the steadiness, the wisdom,
the sanity when all else feels ridiculous

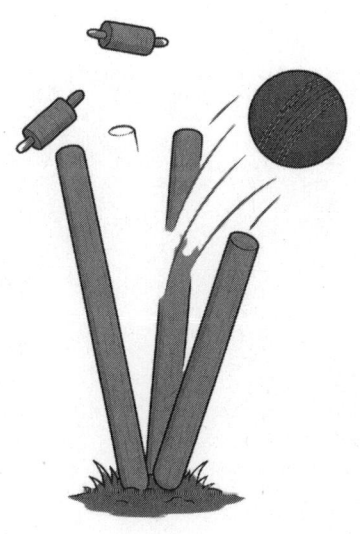

CONTENTS

1

A BRAVE NEW WORLD

JUNE 2025, HEADINGLEY, LEEDS

It might be a strange instinct, but all Shubman can think about right now is how cold the weather is. June back home would mean warmth, almost sweltering heat. Uncomfortable, perhaps, but still good cricketing weather. The wind in Leeds, on the other hand, bites. In its own way, it's not unfamiliar to Shubman. It reminds him of the Punjabi winters of his childhood.

Shubman walks down the dressing room stairs briskly. He's done a good job keeping the promise he made to himself when the announcement first came through: no checking

newspapers and always coming down early for team meetings. The rest of the team trickles down in ones and twos, and they bundle together to hash out the plan for the upcoming match.

This is the inaugural iteration of the Anderson–Tendulkar Trophy, the newly renamed series between India and England. More personally, it marks Shubman's first-ever outing as India's Test captain. There's a fizzy sort of anticipation in the air: The whole world is watching to see how India will perform under its young new captain after the legendary reigns of Virat Kohli and Rohit Sharma.

Shubman, for his part, is trying very hard not to think about it. The plan for the match is in place, his team is well-prepared and honestly unstoppably fierce when they find their rhythm; all he needs to do is what he's always done: trust his team, let them do what they do best, and keep a cool head and play his heart out when he steps up to the crease.

When he is called to the pitch for the toss, it really sinks in: *I'm the captain of the Indian Test team.* It wasn't that long ago when this was Rohit Sharma's kingdom, and it's a bittersweet sort of feeling for Shubman. On the one hand, inheriting the team from a beloved captain is never easy, and the headlines have been too loud since he and Virat Kohli retired. Shubman is young, too, and he'd be lying if he said he hadn't been thinking about his age in terms of seniority, both within the team and outside it. Besides, he's spent his entire career so far playing under the captaincy of Rohit Sharma; it's only natural for it to feel a little weird.

The nerves, the apprehensions, the questions all fade away when the game begins. England win the toss and decide they will bowl first; India take the bat. This is Shubman Gill's first-ever match as India's Test captain, and it's time to play some cricket.

'I love batting for long hours; it gives me confidence.'

— SHUBMAN GILL

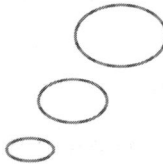

2

THE PLANTING OF A SEED

There's a slight nip in the air when Lakhwinder Singh steps out of his cottage into the crisp, slightly misty morning air. It's Saturday, and there's plenty of work to do on the farm. The first order of business for him, however, is a strong cup of sweet, milky tea, which he sips slowly, letting the warmth seep through him. Lakhwinder draws a deep breath before he begins his morning walk through the fields. Today, only a mild breeze moves the tops of all the crops as he gets to work.

He doesn't notice the passage of time except to note where the sun is in the sky, and before he knows it, the sun is shining overhead and his wife is calling him over for lunch. His two children, Shahneel and Shubman, are already running around the courtyard playing with each other.

Lakhwinder is focused on his meal when he hears his daughter shriek suddenly: 'Papa! Look here! Shubman won't let me play with the bat!' Before his wife, Keart, can respond, go to the children, calm them down and chastise them for interrupting their father's lunchtime, a delighted peal of laughter rings through the air. Lakhwinder can't help it either – he laughs to himself as he washes and dries his hands before making his way out into the courtyard.

The bat is a small one, and Lakhwinder can't quite remember how it had made its way into their house. Perhaps it was a gift from a relative or an enthusiastic neighbour; perhaps it was a souvenir from one of his own trips into the city. When he steps out to see his little boy waving it around like a sword, he can't help the way he stops in his tracks.

It feels like a lifetime ago to Lakhwinder, being the young boy who dreamed of playing cricket for Punjab, maybe even for India. The sweaty days spent running around with his friends, the balls that would eventually, inevitably be worn down, the sharp thwack of bat hitting leather, the peals of laughter, the shouts that rang through the air. Something about young Shubman waving the bat around, trying to understand how to hold it, kindles something like a spark deep in Lakhwinder's chest.

As he returns to the field to resume his work, an idea begins to take shape, slowly, piece by piece. By the time the sun begins to dip, Lakhwinder has a clear plan set out in his mind. He starts by looking for three smooth pebbles, which he easily finds in the farmland. Returning to the courtyard, he sets them up in a straight line before walking back into the cottage.

It takes a while, rooting through old things, before he finds the soft old ball hidden away in

a drawer. He tosses it into the air and catches it, partly out of old habit, partly to remember how it feels. He's still tossing it up into the air when he steps out and calls for Shubman. 'Beta! Where are you? Come here – and bring the bat!'

Shubman waddles over, little bat in tow. 'Yes, Baba!' His voice has the soft, lispy quality that all three-year-old voices have. He giggles as he wobbles his way to his father. Lakhwinder smiles, eyes crinkling, when he sees Shubman. 'All right, come stand here.' He has Shubman take his place in front of the three stones he has placed in a line.

Lakhwinder takes a couple of steps back before gently lobbing the ball to Shubman. A peal of delighted laughter follows as the young boy smacks the ball away, gripping the bat with both hands. Lakhwinder initially plans for the game only to last a couple of minutes, but he can't help notice the intensity that flares in the little boy's eyes, and the firmness with which

he holds the bat. They play late into the night before Lakhwinder picks up his son to put him to bed. Shubman giggles sleepily. 'Can we play again tomorrow?'

'Yes Beta, we'll play again tomorrow,' Lakhwinder mumbles quietly as he takes his son to bed beside his wife. That night, Lakhwinder stays awake a long time thinking to himself, remembering his own childhood. *Tomorrow, we'll play again*, he thinks to himself.

Shubman falls into an easy rhythm with his father as time passes, and neither of them seem to tire of the sport. Lakhwinder doesn't tire of bowling to Shubman, and Shubman, for his part, doesn't tire of hitting the ball. What starts with twenty balls a day slowly grows to fifty, then a hundred. In four years' time, by the time Shubman is seven years old, he's practising on 500–700 balls in a day.

At the time, in the very beginning, for Lakhwinder, Shubman is all potential, all promise.

When Lakhwinder sees his young son, all fierce eyes and brows furrowed in concentration, he remembers his own childhood, his own dreams of becoming a cricketer. However, it doesn't take Lakhwinder long to see the promise in Shubman's stance, the determination in his eyes. The practice is gruelling, and it never stops, come rain, hail or sunshine; but Shubman doesn't give up either.

In their later years, perhaps both Shubman and Lakhwinder remember these days as the foundation to something greater than either of them, the planting of a seed that shows signs of growing into something great, big and fruitful.

'*There is no shortcut to success; you have to put in the work every day.*'

— SHUBMAN GILL

3

MOVIN' ON UPWARDS

The new bat feels heavy in Shubman's palms. The grip is rough, but not unfamiliar, and his hands, calloused as they are, can handle the pressure easily now. It might be a strange sight to the average onlooker. If you were to walk into this little farm in Chak Kherewala, Fazilka, Punjab, you might be surprised, for instance, to see a seven-year-old boy clutching the roughly hewn wooden bat like his life depends on it. You might notice, first, the fiery intensity in his eyes, narrowed in careful, sharp focus.

If you swivelled your line of sight a little, you might turn to see an older man lobbing balls. No matter the time of day, no matter if the sun is beating down on them, no matter if the rain is coming down in sheets, or if the wind is howling through the greenery of the farm.

These daily exercises, undoubtedly repetitive to the average bystander, are a daily staple for father and son. On this particular day, a windy, warm morning in October, Lakhwinder is bowling his trademark short-pitched deliveries. Whenever one comes his way, Shubman jabs his bat forward and sends the ball rolling away.

Lakhwinder is unrelenting in his bowling, and he has noticed how much better his son has become in the last few years. Long gone are the days he would be out of breath after an hour of practice, asking for a water break, or to rest before resuming. Shubman's eyes are keen as he watches each delivery from his father. Depending on where it bounces, Shubman steps forward to smack it away, or takes a quick step back to knock it away.

Shubman's batting wasn't always this accurate, but his father's dedicated training has allowed him to become an excellent judge of the ball. He now instinctively seems to know what to do with a delivery: If it pitches short, he knows to jab at it to send it rolling to the boundary; if the ball pitches off the stump, he knows to leave it be instead of rising to the bait; if it bounces too close to his feet, he already knows to scoop it away to protect the stumps.

Shubman isn't the only one to notice how much easier batting has become for him; his father pays attention to it too – how much faster Shubman is to respond to his deliveries, how much sharper, more technically sound his batting has become.

There is nothing particularly special about this day. Lakhwinder is doing what he always does: He takes his place at one end of the home-made pitch on the farm, takes a short run-up, and tosses the ball at Shubman, who hits it away for

what would easily have been a boundary on a real cricket ground. Lakhwinder doesn't think much of it – other than to shout 'good shot!' – as he bowls his next ball. Except Shubman does it again, on a shorter delivery this time, smacking it away for a would-be boundary.

This happens over and over, until Lakhwinder has bowled over twenty balls, each slightly more aggressive, slightly trickier than the last. Shubman, for his part, doesn't stop, doesn't miss and doesn't let the stumps fall. Lakhwinder doesn't stop, but he does notice the quiet confidence that seems to have seeped into Shubman's stance. It's evident in the way he holds the bat, takes his position, even when he taps the ground with his bat as the ball comes at him.

Later, when they take a break to drink water and wipe the sweat off their brows, Lakhwinder will call Shubman to him: 'Are you doing something different today?' Shubman will

shake his head: 'No, Baba, just what I always do.' Lakhwinder will consider chalking it up to a good batting day, but something about the determined look in Shubman's eyes will stop him from dismissing the day.

The next day, this will happen again. And the day after that.

The year is 2007, and Shubman Gill, simply put, seems to have outgrown his training on the farm at long last. He doesn't quite notice yet, but as his mother watches him practice, standing on the threshold of their home, a dupatta over her head to shield her face from the sun, she notices how much easier it comes to him, the dance of batting, than it used to even a year earlier.

The stars are twinkling up in the sky, and a light, chilly breeze is blowing through the farm. Lakhwinder and Keart are walking, heads put together, lost deep in their conversation.

'I think he's outgrown practising on the farm.' Lakhwinder's eyes are furrowed thoughtfully.

'There was a time he'd struggle to predict what the ball would do; I see him having no such trouble now.'

Keart nods, and she can't keep the pride out of her voice when she responds: 'He held his wicket all through yesterday; not a single miss.'

'I think it's time to consider Mohali again. I know we had decided it was too soon last year, but a lot has changed since then.' Lakhwinder turns to look at Keart. 'We always knew this day was coming.'

The discussion between Lakhwinder and Keart is an old one in the Gill household. A few years ago, while watching Shubman practice on the makeshift pitch Lakhwinder had made at the farm, he had begun to think to himself: *This may be a workable short-term solution, but proper training will mean proper facilities.*

After a lot of thought and many conversations – about money, logistics, education, timing – a conclusion had been reached: When Shubman is old enough, and ready for the pressure, the family would move to Mohali, to be near the famed Punjab Cricket Association (PCA) stadium in Mohali.

Keart and Lakhwinder walk a while longer, talking about the logistics of it all: The move would mean a school transfer for Shahneel and Shubman; moving costs for the family's furniture, a conversation with the kids' grandparents, who would stay back to take care of the farm, and perhaps most importantly, a discussion with Shubman to prepare him for what is to come.

When they break the news to Shubman a few days later, he's over the moon. The preparations are done, and thus, the Gill family sets off to make itself a new home in Mohali, Punjab. On some level, deep in his heart, Shubman understands this is all for him: His family is going to great lengths to ensure he has access

to the kind of training that can make him a true cricketer, giving him a fighting chance to wear India's bright blue jersey.

As the family piles into the train to make the 300 kilometre journey from Chak Kherewala to Mohali, and Shubman takes his place in the window seat, he makes himself a promise:

I will do my very best — anything less is simply no longer acceptable.

— SHUBMAN GILL

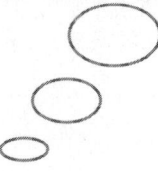

4

A PRINCE IS BORN

All things considered, it wasn't easy for Lakhwinder and Keart to up and move their entire lives from Fazilka to Mohali. That said, they didn't second-guess themselves even once, they knew that if Shubman was to play for India as Lakhwinder had once dreamed of doing himself, this was the only way. After all, Mohali was much closer to the heart of Punjab's cricket; the PCA's stadium was here, as were the state-of-the-art training facilities. For Shahneel and Shubman, too, the adjustment took a while, but soon, the family settled into their new lives.

Shubman, too, dreamed the same dream as his father; he was fuelled by the same sense of determination and refusal to give up, no matter the hardship that came before him. This has been true when he was a child, training in the farmlands of Fazilka, and it's true now, as he trains in the famed grounds of Punjab's cricketing infrastructure.

The year is 2010. An All India Pace Bowlers' Camp is being organized by the PCA. The idea is simple: state cricket associations all over the country organize camps to train their young players and identify promising talent that can be honed to play for the state at the domestic level, and if all goes well, eventually, to represent India. The PCA is no different, and it has invited pace bowlers from all over the country to participate. If you perform well, not only will you get a chance to benefit from the camp, you also get to play alongside the best the state has to offer. If you get really lucky, maybe the right coach, trainer or selector will spot you and remember.

Karsan Devjibhai Ghavri, a legendary left-arm fast-medium pace bowler, and one of the earliest cricketing icons of Team India, played for India from 1974 to 1981, including the 1975 and 1979 World Cups. On that day in 2010, however, Ghavri is in Mohali to oversee the All India Pace Bowlers' Camp, which is off to a good start: Ghavri and a small team of coaches have already instructed the boys to warm up, and done an extensive physical training session that lasted all morning. The boys have collected in small groups of twos and threes and were drinking water, mopping the sweat off their faces, when Ghavri notices a serious wrench in the plans for the day.

It is time for the pace bowlers to begin their practice in the nets – one of the most important parts of the camp, when aspiring young bowlers actually get the chance to show off what they can do with the actual ball. However, there is a problem: How is a bowler to demonstrate what they can do if there is no one to bowl at? Even as the bowlers get ready to practice in the nets, Ghavri realizes there are no batters standing by. He quickly calls Mahender Pandove and Sushil Kapoor, the managers of Punjab's Ranji team, and points the problem out to them. To their credit, they very quickly find a solution and call for some batters.

As the camp goes on, it begins to drizzle, and the session has to be moved indoors. As the boys from the camp mill about to get inside, Ghavri calls on one of his assistant coaches: 'Let's take a walk while we wait for the nets session to resume.' The drizzle is pleasant and the weather nice, so it seems like a perfect way to while some time away. As Ghavri and his assistant coach begin to walk around, they notice peals of laughter and shouting in the distance. When you've been a cricketer for as long as someone like Ghavri has been, the one sound you know better than your own breath is the sound of a great cricket match in progress,

and that's exactly what these distant sounds seem to suggest. Both men shoot each other a knowing look as they walk towards the field.

They reach the nearby ground in a matter of minutes, and what they see stuns them. Paying no heed whatsoever to the steady drizzle that has begun to come down, a gaggle of twelve- and thirteen-year-old boys are playing, and one particularly lanky young boy is batting with serious finesse. Ghavri can't help but notice him: the way he moves with the bat like it is an extension of his arm, his body; his stance; the sharp, canny anticipation with which he chooses his shots as the bowler comes at him.

Ghavri stands awhile, transfixed alongside his assistant coach as he watches the young boy bat. Eventually, a particularly loud shout from one of the boys shakes him out of his stupor. The boy's batting is, honestly, like watching poetry take physical form. But if Ghavri wants to do something with this bright new discovery, he needs to find out who the boy is. He shoots

a look at his assistant coach, who smiles at him with shining eyes. Almost as if they are both united by the same thought, they both move in opposite directions and begin to ask the people around if they know who the boy is, but nobody seems to know.

After half an hour of this, as the rains come to a stop, and it is time for Ghavri to return to his camp, he begins the walk back to the nets. On his way to exit the field, he notices a tall man with sharp, kind eyes standing under the shade of a tree, watching the match closely. Something in his bones tells him to speak to the man, and Ghavri has never been a man to shy away from his instincts. When they begin to talk, the man tells Ghavri his son is batting. Ghavri glances over at the boy, and realizes with a shock that it is the very same boy whose name they wanted to know. Shubman Gill.

Ghavri turns to Lakhwinder: 'Your son is an excellent batter; I think he has the potential to be a fantastic cricketer. Will you send him to the

PCA nets tomorrow?' Lakhwinder immediately agrees, but Ghavri is not quite done. 'We have a pace bowling camp going on at the PCA. I know your son's a batter, and he's young, but I think I'd like to see what he can do against our pacers.' What Ghavri doesn't – or perhaps can't – articulate at the time is that deep in his heart, he truly believes Shubman can face the eighteen-year-olds in the nets.

The next day, Shubman arrives at the PCA nets to face the participants of the All India Pace Bowling Camp. Years later, Karsan Ghavri would recall: 'He was fantastic. For a twelve-year-old, he played straight and was not afraid of pace. They even bowled bouncers, but he wasn't terrified.'

While the camp is designed to find pacers for the PCA, what it does end up giving them is a batter who would make history. After that first day, Shubman is told to attend the camp every day. As Ghavri watches him put his hard yards in, day after day, he is impressed beyond words. Later, he would go on to find Mr Pandove, Punjab's Ranji team manager, to strongly recommend that Shubman Gill be placed in Punjab's U-14 team. The rest, as they say, is history.

When asked about the camp years later, and whether, all of twelve years old, he was scared of being hit by the ball, this is what Shubman had to say,

'Once you get hit by a ball, the fear of getting hurt goes away.'

— SHUBMAN GILL

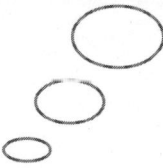

5

DOMESTIC SALAD DAYS

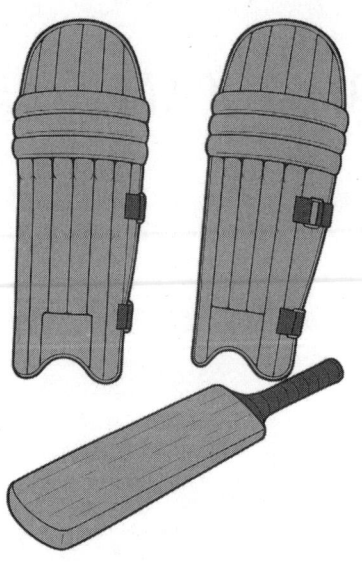

Throughout his time playing domestic cricket for Punjab, Shubman becomes fast friends with another young batting prodigy: the young, bright-eyed Abhishek Sharma. They meet in a U-14 camp while playing for Punjab and go on to open for Punjab together.

When the team travels for matches together, Shubman and Abhishek inevitably end up as roommates, a tradition that continues throughout their days of playing together for Punjab. They are found stuck to each other so often that they have to be separated during travel and play, because the coaches quickly realize that if these two young boys are left to their own devices, they'd speak to absolutely no one else on the team.

Years later, when Shubman makes his T20 captaincy debut against Zimbabwe, Abhishek makes his India debut under him.

FEBRUARY 2017, FEROZ SHAH KOTLA, NEW DELHI – THE VIJAY HAZARE TROPHY

February in Delhi – well, all of north India – is great cricketing weather. The chill of the winter is seeping away slowly, and the sun actually feels quite pleasant when you step up to bat in one of India's oldest cricket stadiums. However, Shubman isn't really enjoying the weather. He's thinking about the last time he was called up to play in the Vijay Hazare Trophy, India's premier domestic tournament in the one-day format, and how he was run out for 11 in the match against Vidarbha.

As he steps on to the crease in only his second List A match, he's thinking only one thing really:

Play it cool, and stay on the wicket. The thing about cricket is that when you've been playing for as long as someone like Shubman has, your body does all the thinking for you. After a certain point, you learn to lean into the instinct that tells you *this ball is going to swing outwards*, or *he's going to bowl a yorker*. When you choose not to listen to that instinct, you do so at your own risk.

The real question in moments like this is: How do you know to trust what you feel in your bones? The answer: years of practice, the way Shubman has put in his entire life. So, while there's a small, niggling worry at the back of his head that says *what if you get out again like last time*, he ignores it. This, too, comes with practice.

Ignoring the voice serves him well, because Shubman scores the first List A century of his career against Assam.

INDIAN EXPRESS

HELMET REMOVED and bat raised, a jaded Shubman Gill walked back to the dressing room to a thunderous applause and a standing ovation from his Punjab teammates. It was a pleasant afternoon at Delhi's Feroz Shah Kotla, but Shubman was drenched in sweat, and his bright blue jersey soiled with mud.

This was special. This was a moment that would be etched in his memory forever.

DECEMBER 2018, PCA STADIUM, MOHALI, PUNJAB – THE RANJI TROPHY

Another winter, another great cricketing day. Shubman feels it humming in his bones: It's going to be a good day for him. Punjab already has a 264-run lead in the first innings, but that doesn't necessarily let Shubman rest easy. Punjab has a strong side, with Yuvraj Singh and Gurkeerat Singh Mann in the team, but on the fourth day of the Ranji Trophy match against Tamil Nadu, it is Shubman Gill who shines brighter than all who came before him. He bats for over 300 balls, and as each one comes at him in the second innings of the match, he thinks of his father bowling to him endlessly back home in Fazilka.

Shubman doesn't know this when he steps up to the crease, but when he walks away, out at 268 runs, he has made his first-ever double-century in cricket while playing for Punjab, against a fierce bowling side in Tamil Nadu, where the wily spinner Sai Kishore has already taken 6 wickets.

> '*I always try to learn from every innings, whether I score big or get out early.*'
>
> — SHUBMAN GILL

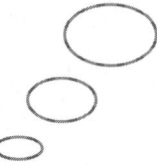

6

CLASS OF 2018:
THE U–19 WORLD CUP

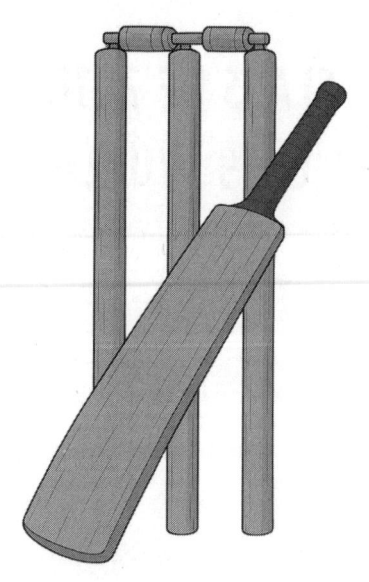

DECEMBER 2017, PUNJAB

It's a time of great tension and anticipation in the Gill household. The squad list for the ICC's U-19 World Cup is set to be announced any day now. Shubman has had an excellent year on the domestic circuit. He has already made for an excellent Ranji Trophy player, and his record playing List A cricket – the one-day or 50 overs a side format – has been excellent. The house is thrumming with excitement: Everyone's hoping Shubman's name will be on the squad list, but it's all hope at the moment.

After all, cricket is not a game of guarantees. While Shubman's performance has been steady and reliable in the domestic circuit so far, it's a not a guarantee of anything, least of all a chance to wear the India blue.

Which is why when the list is announced in the press on 3 December, the first feeling in the Gill family is one of relief, followed by celebration. Shubman checks the squad list on the computer in the study of the house, refreshing the BCCI's website until the press release finally, *finally* appears.

'Ma! Baba!' Shubman shouts. 'The squad list is out. I'm vice-captain!' The house erupts in celebration. Yes, everyone was hoping for Shubman's selection, but seeing it printed, officially, that the promising young cricketer Shubman Gill will be vice-captaining India in the prestigious ICC U-19 World Cup is a relief indeed. It's confirmation, in many ways, of all

ICC U-19 WORLD CUP
SQUAD LIST

PRITHVI SHAW (C)

SHUBMAN GILL (VC)

HARVIK DESAI (WK)

ARYAN JUYAL (WK)

MANJOT KALRA

SHIVAM MAVI

KAMLESH NAGARKOTI

RIYAN PARAG

ISHAN POREL

HIMANSHU RANA

ANUKUL ROY

ARSHDEEP SINGH

SHIVA SINGH

ADITYA THAKARE

the hard work Shubman has put into his cricket his entire life.

It doesn't take him long to go find the phone to call his best friend Abhishek, who he will be playing alongside in the tournament. There are other names he recognizes: Prithvi Shaw, their captain, a sharp, talented powerhouse of a player from Mumbai; Aryan Juyal, the sharp wicket-keeper-batter from Uttar Pradesh; Shivam Mavi, Shiva Singh, both excellent players from Uttar Pradesh; and Abhishek Sharma and Arshdeep Singh from his own state team.

A month later, India's U-19 team flies to New Zealand to compete in the tournament under the watchful mentorship of Rahul Dravid, and Shubman Gill announces his arrival on the international stage with a thrilling batting run at the tournament.

11 JANUARY 2018, SOMEWHERE IN NEW ZEALAND

It has been a long training session – sharp drills under the New Zealand sun, Rahul Dravid watching with the same intensity he used to bring to his playing days.

It is Rahul sir's birthday, and for once, cricket isn't the main item on the agenda. Not officially.

In the hotel hallway after dinner, Shubman, Abhishek and Kamlesh huddle like conspirators, whispering over a boxed chocolate cake that looks far too innocent for what they are planning.

'We're doing it,' Shubman says, eyes gleaming with mischief. Kamlesh is already holding the cake at an angle, and Abhishek has grabbed tissue paper.

'We'll have to be really fast,' Abhishek says, all serious eyes and determination.

When Dravid walks in – calm, smiling politely, wearing the expression of a man politely prepared to be sung 'Happy Birthday' to

and then left alone – he doesn't stand a chance. There is the song, of course. The clapping. The awkward team chorus. Then, in an instant, in a blink-and-you'll-miss-it sort of way, Shubman and Abhishek lunge forward, Kamlesh right behind them.

The cake lands squarely on Rahul Dravid's face.

For a fraction of a second, the room is completely still. A pause. A flicker of fear. Then Dravid starts laughing, a deep, surprised, slightly helpless laugh that no one in that room had quite heard before. Relief and celebration reign over the room in equal measure that day.

14 JANUARY 2018, MOUNT MAUNGANUI, NEW ZEALAND. THE FIRST MATCH OF THE TOURNAMENT. INDIA U–19 VS AUSTRALIA U–19

Mount Maunganui, with its gentle coastal breeze and lush outfield, has the air of a holiday town.

But in the dressing room, the environment is quite different. The Indian squad is quiet. Focused.

Shubman walks out to bat at number 3, moments after the fall of the first wicket. It's not nerves he feels, not exactly; it's something sharper. He has played on turning tracks, on dead pitches, on cold mornings in Punjab and under searing lights in domestic tournaments. But this is different.

This is the U-19 World Cup. And the jersey on his back no longer says 'Punjab'. It says 'India'.

He composes himself. Then he starts. The shots are clean. Precise. The kind of batting that looks less like risk-taking and more like poetry, unfolding slowly, but also inevitably. By the time he's done, he has 63 runs to his name, scored off 54 deliveries.

Later that evening, the captain Prithvi Shaw tells him it looked like he'd been batting on that pitch for years. Shubman just shrugs. He's already thinking about the next game.

30 JANUARY 2018, CHRISTCHURCH, NEW ZEALAND. THE SEMI-FINAL. INDIA VS PAKISTAN

Outside the stadium, the flags wave, the anthems play, and the broadcast teams talk in hushed tones. Inside the dressing room, the players stretch and wait. Shubman is calm. He knows what this match means – not just for India, not just for the team, but for him.

This is the biggest match he has played in his life so far. It is also, in many ways, the most familiar. There is a silence in him, a kind of tunnel vision. It's not that the crowd disappears, it's that it becomes background noise, like the wind in the trees.

Shubman's footwork is crisp, his movement impeccable, his placement tidy. Every run builds more and more pressure on the fielding side. He finishes the innings with 102* runs off 94 balls. Unbeaten. Unshaken. Unmissable.

When the team huddles around him after the win – with a crushing 203-run margin – Rahul

Dravid pulls him aside. He doesn't say much. He doesn't have to.

3 FEBRUARY 2018, TAURANGA, NEW ZEALAND. THE FINAL. INDIA VS AUSTRALIA, AGAIN

The beginning feels familiar, but the stakes are higher, and the crowd feels larger than life. Shubman doesn't have his best innings today – 31 runs off 30 balls – but the team doesn't need him to be the hero this time. Manjot Kalra scores a stunning century, and the bowlers do their job with lethality.

Still, Shubman can't quite help himself; he watches the match with intent, every muscle tuned to the tension of the game. When the final run is scored, and the Indian bench clears in a rush of joy, he lets himself smile. Just a little. Not because he's surprised, but because he isn't.

He finishes the tournament with 372 runs, the most by any batter, and becomes Player of the

Tournament. In the press room, someone asks him what this tournament means to him. He says something polite, modest, measured. But later, back in his hotel room, when he takes off the India jersey and sets it down on the bed, he looks at it for a long time before folding it carefully.

This is just the beginning, he thinks to himself.

> '*Every time I walk out to bat, I carry the hopes and dreams of my team and my country with me.*'
>
> — SHUBMAN GILL

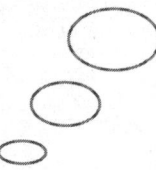

7

THE BIG BOOK OF ACHIEVEMENTS

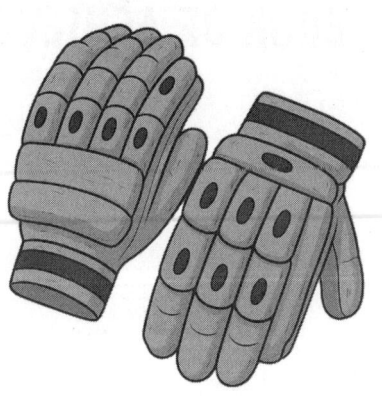

31 JANUARY 2019, HAMILTON, NEW ZEALAND, FOURTH ODI, INDIA VS NEW ZEALAND

Before his ODI debut for India, he seems to hear this constantly: from senior players, coaching staff, even his own friends. Everyone keeps telling him it's going to feel different, it's going to change who he is. Shubman doesn't quite know what to make of it – all things considered, he's been playing for years now – until he steps onto the field himself.

The first thing he notices is that the silence feels different now. There's a hush in the dressing room, there's a hush on the team bus. It's almost like there's a certain kind of silence that follows you into your first international match. Not nerves – well, not *just* nerves – but something more distilled. A hum that seems to run in his blood, reside in his mind, saying just one thing: *focus.*

At Seddon Park in Hamilton, Shubman walks out in an India jersey for the first time. It's not the under-19 blue. It's not India A. This one fits perfectly, like all the jerseys that came before it, of course, but it seems to feel heavier, somehow. The fabric feels stiff across his shoulders, not quite broken in yet. New kit. New chapter.

He's nineteen. His name's been on people's lips for over a year now. *U-19 World Cup hero. IPL prodigy. The next one. The Prince.* But here, in front of the New Zealand crowd and a sky as pale as a white ball in winter, none of that matters. Here, there are only deliveries, field placements and expectations that arrive with a number next to your name.

India is struggling. The top order has crumbled. He comes in at number 3, a familiar position to him by now, but he steps onto

unfamiliar terrain. He faces his first few balls cautiously. There's swing. There's bounce. There's also Trent Boult, and he isn't here to hand out warm welcomes.

Shubman makes 9 runs off 21 balls before falling. A short stay, not one for the record books. But when he walks back, head level, gloves tucked under one arm, there's no sense of defeat. Just unfinished business.

Later, in the dressing room, someone pats him on the back and says, 'First one's always like this.' He nods. He already knows the next one will be different.

19 JANUARY 2021, BRISBANE, AUSTRALIA, FOURTH TEST, BORDER—GAVASKAR TROPHY, THE GABBA

The Gabba is loud. Even with restricted capacity, even in the middle of the pandemic, the Gabba feels loud. It's not the people. Well, it's not just the people. It's like every inch of the stands, the field,

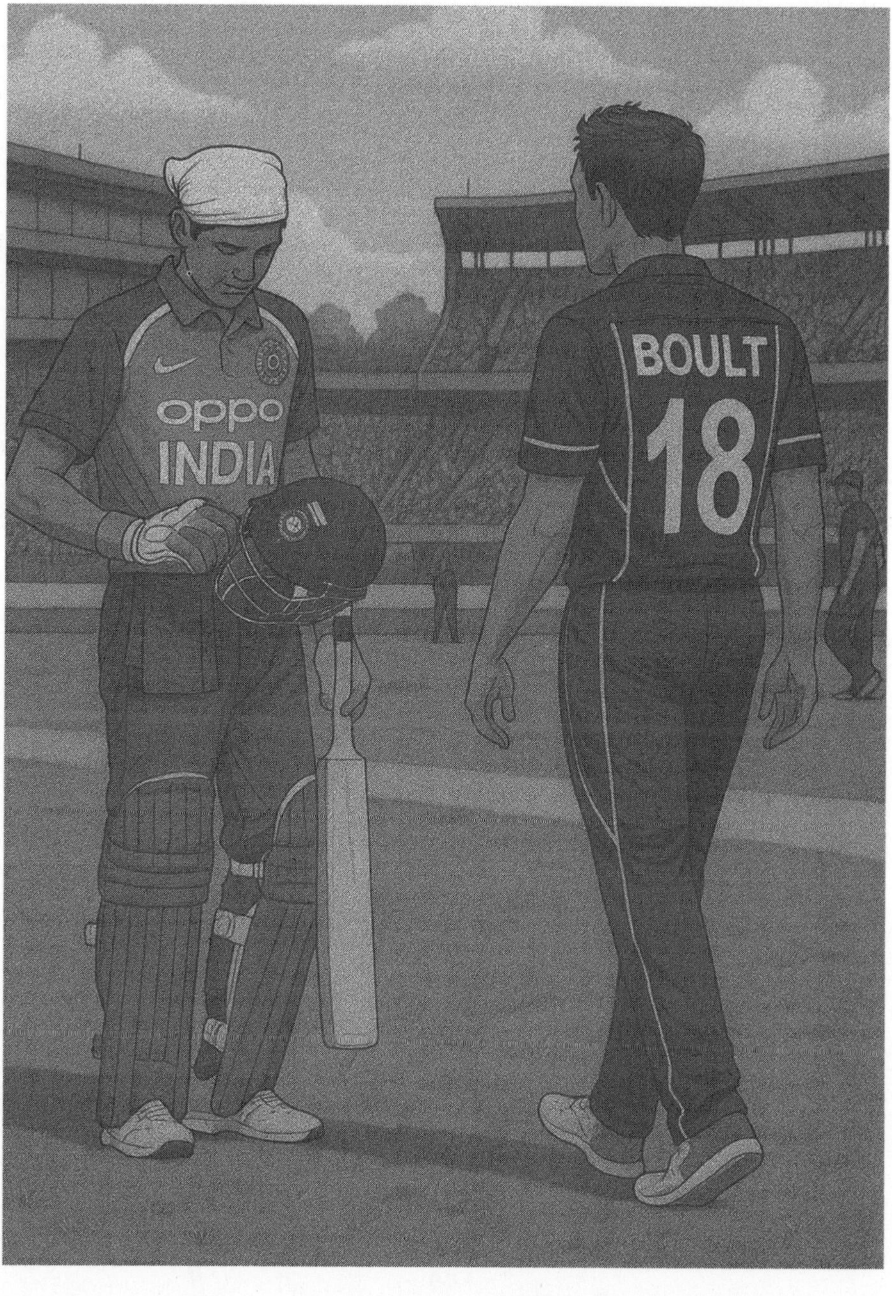
oppo
INDIA
BOULT
18

the pitch, even the dressing room, hums with the weight of history. It's like the Gabba – often called Australia's cricketing fortress – hums with the weight of its own reputation.

Thirty-two years. That's how long it's been since Australia last lost a Test match at this ground. The commentators have said it. The press has printed it. The players have heard it, over and over again. India is chasing 328 runs on the final day. The series is tied. The series is bruised. The team is held together by tape, teenagers and something tougher than resilience.

Shubman walks in after the early fall of Rohit Sharma. The surface is still playing true, but there's something jagged about the moment. Nathan Lyon is eyeing the rough. Pat Cummins is already steaming in it. It doesn't feel like a chase; it feels like the team is fighting for survival.

And then Shubman plays that shot. Outside off, just short of a length, and suddenly it's flying through point, too fast for the field to matter. His hands move before the crowd can inhale. Not a flourish. Not an accident.

The innings that follows from Shubman's bat builds quietly. Drives. Cuts. The occasional pull. No celebration. He crosses 50, then 60. Then 80. Australia begin to shift uneasily.

Shubman ultimately falls for 91, just short of a century. That day, however, it doesn't need to be one. When he bows before the crowd, bat held behind his back – a celebration he will come to be known for – the world already knows it's the kind of innings people remember longer than a hundred. The kind of innings that changes the shape of a match, and maybe a career.

India goes on to win – against the odds, against the noise, against the Gabba. The fortress falls at last. And somewhere in the middle of it, a twenty-one-year-old from Punjab

knows, deep in his bones, that he has helped rewrite history with a bat in hand.

18 JANUARY 2023, HYDERABAD, INDIA. FIRST ODI, INDIA VS NEW ZEALAND

Shubman has always thought there is something different about the light in Hyderabad in January. The sky is cloudless, the outfield fast. It's the kind of day that doesn't suggest history will be made. Just cricket, as usual. It's a good day to play some cricket.

But Shubman Gill stands at the crease as if the day is already his. There is no early rush, no mindless chase for runs or domination. No signs of tension. It's easy, and that's how Shubman approaches it. He takes his time. The first ten runs arrive like footsteps on a familiar path. The bat feels light today, like an extension of his arm, as it sometimes does when everything else is in sync.

By the time he reaches his half-century, the crowd is beginning to lean forward. The movement in his shots is crisp, but never hurried. He has always had timing, but today, he decides he's going to take his time. When the century comes, his third in ODIs, he doesn't celebrate wildly. Just a glance to the sky, his trademark smile, his trademark bow. On that day, however, he isn't done.

What happens next is pure intent in action. Everything outside off is punished. Anything short disappears. A full toss is whipped through midwicket without hesitation. Shubman isn't being aggressive, not really. He's just playing as he often does, leaning into instinct and assurance, and the result: He plays like he's inevitable.

At 150, the crowd is roaring. At 180, they're on their feet. When he finally reaches 200, he raises his bat, helmet off, and takes a bow again. 208 runs. The youngest-ever to reach a

double century in ODIs. The fifth Indian to do it. Records are mentioned, replayed, tweeted, archived. But in the moment, standing under the Hyderabad sky, sweat on his brow, bat resting lightly in his hand, Shubman just breathes.

JUNE 2024, HARARE, ZIMBABWE. INDIA VS ZIMBABWE, FIVE-MATCH T20I SERIES

By now, the flights have come to feel like routine to Shubman. The training sessions, the press days, the jerseys with his name on the back all feel familiar, all carry the scent of the everyday for him. But this tour is different. This time, he's not just part of the squad. He's leading it.

Shubman Gill, twenty-four, is named captain of the Indian team for the tour of Zimbabwe. It's not the full-strength side. Some senior players are resting. But it's still the Indian team. And his name comes first on the team sheet. He doesn't say much when the news breaks. A short statement. A few words about opportunity,

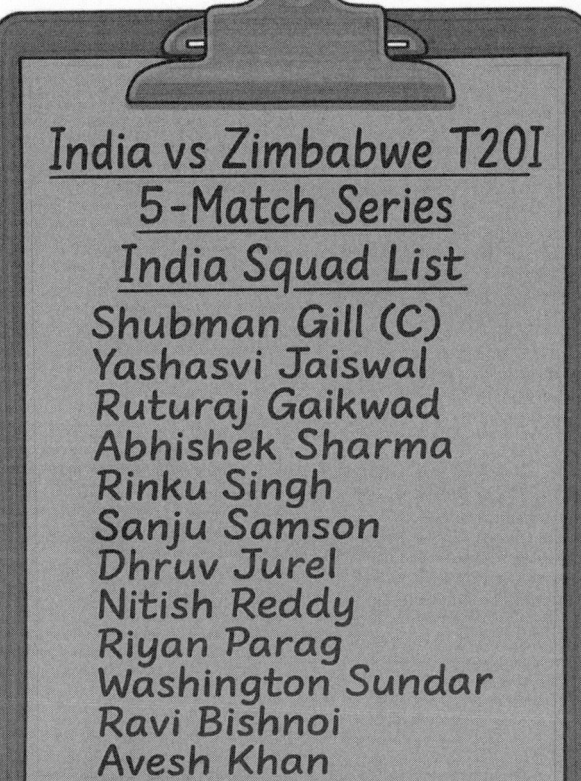

India vs Zimbabwe T20I
5-Match Series
India Squad List

Shubman Gill (C)
Yashasvi Jaiswal
Ruturaj Gaikwad
Abhishek Sharma
Rinku Singh
Sanju Samson
Dhruv Jurel
Nitish Reddy
Riyan Parag
Washington Sundar
Ravi Bishnoi
Avesh Khan
Khaleel Ahmed
Mukesh Kumar
Tushar Deshpande

pride, focus. The kind of things a captain is supposed to say.

But in his head, he's remembering other firsts – his debut in Hamilton, the 91 at the Gabba, the double century in Hyderabad. And now, this.

The series itself is competitive. Zimbabwe push back harder than expected. India still win 4–1.

Shubman, for his part, is measured. Not flashy. The field changes are thoughtful, calculated. His own batting is composed, anchored. There's no single standout innings – just presence. Stability.

He's still learning. He knows that. Leadership is less about one moment and more about how you carry the people around you.

When he returns home, the series doesn't make headlines. No parades. No trophy photos on front pages. But in the team's WhatsApp group, there are quiet congratulations. A few emojis. A nod from the seniors. And that's enough. For now.

Because a boy who once waited for his name on a squad list – refreshing the BCCI website alone in his study – is now the one writing names into the line-up.

And this, too, is only the beginning.

> 'When you represent your country, there is no fatigue. It was my dream to play for India, and I am very fortunate to be a part of the team in all three formats.'
>
> — SHUBMAN GILL

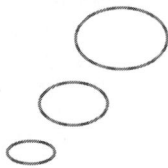

8

THE ANNOUNCEMENT

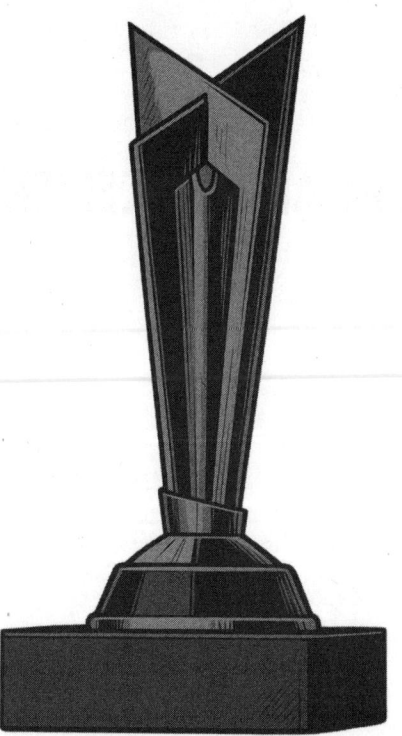

MAY 2025

It's late in the evening. Indian fans are still warmly swaddled in the memory of the Champions Trophy win, and honestly, other than the country buzzing in anticipation for the IPL, nothing much is actually happening in the world of cricket.

Until.

The multicoloured Instagram circle showing a new story appears around Rohit Sharma's profile, announcing his retirement from Test cricket. It happens suddenly; he calls his journey in whites 'an absolute honour'.

A few days later, Virat Kohli posts a photograph of himself in his Test kit.

The usual fuss and chaos of the Indian press and fans follow. Two of Indian cricket's longest-serving names have stepped away. The space they leave behind is not about skill or talent, not really. It's emotional. It's love – what the fans have for them, and what they have for the game.

Only a few weeks later, the BCCI confirms Shubman as India's new Test captain in a much-anticipated press conference just ahead of the five-match series against England, now known as the Anderson–Tendulkar Trophy. The board officials speak of his temperament, his maturity, his ability to grow into the role.

Later, Shubman will receive a short message from Virat, a warm welcome when he arrives in England next month. Then one from Rohit. No advice. Just respect. The rest of the day passes like any other. Training. Strategy meetings. Logistics. But when he goes to sleep that night, there's a cap, navy blue, crested, perfectly

folded, sitting on the table by his bed. And this time, it's not just the cap of a player. It's the cap of a captain.

Shubman doesn't really post anything on social media. Doesn't call his friends, doesn't celebrate, really. Not at first. He sits with his family. When he does speak publicly for the first time after the announcement, his words are careful. Grateful, but steady.

He speaks of learning. Of responsibility. Of the kind of cricket that isn't about being loud or aggressive or angry, but simply about staying in it.

And for the first time in a long while, the future doesn't feel theoretical. It has a name. And it's already inscribed in whites.

'Each and every practice session counts and matters. Before every practice session you should know why are you going for practice, what is your aim and that is what I do – have purposeful practice sessions.'

— SHUBMAN GILL

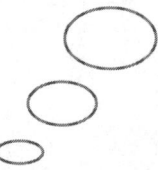

9

DRAWING THE FUTURE

20 JUNE 2025, HEADINGLEY, LEEDS, FIRST TEST, DAY 1

The pitch at Headingley is still fresh – a touch of grass, a trace of swing. The morning air thrums with anticipation. Everyone seems to expect Shubman to be afraid; he's feeling a lot of things, but not fear. Not today. Not for Shubman.

India has lost an early wicket, and then another, but Shubman stays at the crease, unmoved. He plays through the first hour as if the match has already been decided. His cover drive is measured, textbook, beautiful. His defence is tight, compact. There is nothing urgent about the way he is batting today. It's a dance to music only he can hear.

By stumps, Shubman is unbeaten on 127, and India is at 359/3. A first-day dream. The scorecard carries his name in bold, but in the dressing room, he doesn't say much. Just a nod, a quick debrief. The job is far, far from done.

Two days later, India lose the match.

No collapse. No drama. Just slow shifts in momentum, a few chances missed, England digging in longer than expected. In the post-match conference, someone asks Shubman if the century feels bittersweet. He gives a small smile.

'These things balance out,' he says. 'You stay patient.'

Shubman Gill becomes the fifth Indian captain to score a century on debut.

2 JULY 2025, EDGBASTON, BIRMINGHAM, SECOND TEST, DAY 1

Rain has swept through the morning, but the outfield has dried quickly. The light feels stubborn. It's not necessarily bad light – Test

cricket is never played under floodlights, only natural light – it just can't seem to make up its mind. India has been asked to bat.

Shubman walks out slowly. He takes a moment at the crease, adjusts his helmet and settles into his stance. The first few overs pass without hurry. The scoreboard ticks away quietly, keeping numbers, recording history. Another wicket falls. Shubman stays on the crease.

By the end of the day, Shubman walks back unbeaten again, 114 not out, India at 310/5. The applause is polite, a little weary. Birmingham has seen this before. He has made a hundred here once already. Now he has made two.

Back-to-back centuries in his first two Tests as captain.

Shubman's post-match answer is brief: 'Still a long way to go in this series.'

The day ends with the quiet sound of a bat being returned, carefully, to its place, before another day's play.

8 JULY 2025, EDGBASTON, AGAIN, SECOND TEST, DAY 4

The innings has stretched. Not dragged, Shubman never bats like he is dragging anything, but it has extended, slowly, through the hours.

Shubman had started on Day 2 and is astonishingly, astoundingly, still standing. The scorecard says 269 off 387 balls. His first double-century in Tests. His highest score. The highest ever by an Indian captain. The third-highest by an Indian abroad.

There is no turning point – no dropped catch, no sudden acceleration. Just control. Footwork. Patience. Every shot built on the one before it.

In the second innings, he makes 161 more. Two centuries in the same Test. 430 runs in a match, second only to Graham Gooch.

The numbers will come later. The comparisons. The records. Allan Border. Azharuddin. Dravid.

But on the final day, as the team gather around for a quiet cooldown and a late team meeting, Shubman takes a moment to sit apart,

one hand resting on a bottle of water. The other still wrapped in tape from the second innings.

For now, the job is done. And he has done it the only way he knows how to – by staying in.

4 AUGUST 2025, THE OVAL, LONDON, FIFTH TEST, FINAL DAY

The margin is 11 runs.

It is not often that Test cricket delivers a finish like this, not in England, not with the Anderson–Tendulkar Trophy tied, not with India 1 wicket away from the win, and one hit away from losing the match – and the series.

England need 11 runs. India need 1 wicket. Mohammad Siraj has the ball. Gus Atkinson is on strike. Chris Woakes, shoulder dislocated, playing with one arm, stands at the non-striker's end. And for a full hour, tension buzzes in the air. It doesn't feel like cricket. It feels like something else. Something ancient.

There have been dropped catches, missed chances, moments of doubt. But also 8 wickets for Prasidh Krishna, relentless overs from Akash Deep and a stunning 4 wickets to Siraj's name. The fielders have barely spoken. Shubman doesn't move an inch from slip.

Shubman has spent most of the morning standing still, watching, adjusting, waiting. It is the kind of final day that gives you no sense of what is about to happen. Only that it could be anything.

And then, finally, it happens.

A yorker. 143 kmph. Cross-seam. Into the base of off stump. The sound comes first, the crack of timber, perfect silence for a moment, just one moment, and then the stadium erupts. Arms go up. Stumps are pulled from the ground. Siraj, leaping to celebrate. Shubman, sprinting in from the slip cordon, shouting something no one can quite hear.

India has won the match by 6 runs. The series is drawn: 2–2.

No one in the dressing room feels like they've come in second.

Later, when asked about it, about the pressure, the nerves, the risk of losing, Shubman will simply say: 'Such moments make you feel that the journey is worth it.'

> 'Patience is very important, especially in Test cricket.'
>
> — SHUBMAN GILL

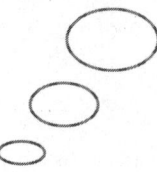

10

SHUBMAN GILL: THE MAN

Shubman Gill was born on 8 September 1999, in Fazilka, Punjab, to Lakhwinder Singh, a farmer who wanted to be a cricketer himself. His favourite toy as a child was a cricket bat.

His father's unique training method taught him to play deliveries that pitched short really well.

Because he would spend so much time practicing, Shubman often didn't get a lot of time to study as a child.

His first-ever cricket bat was made by his grandfather using a tree trunk.

Shubman Gill is one of the Indian cricket team's youngest captains – fifth in a list of players like Mansur Ali Khan Pataudi, Sachin Tendulkar, Kapil Dev and Ravi Shastri.

Shubman is also called 'The Prince' and is known for a unique batting motion that looks like a jab. It's a special type of pull shot that has become his signature, honed due to his father's training method.

Alongside being India's Test captain, Shubman Gill is also the captain of an IPL team, the Gujarat Titans.

Besides playing cricket, Shubman Gill also voiced Pavitra Prabhakar in the famous Spiderman film *Across the Spider-Verse*.

Shubman's cricketing idols are Virat Kohli and Sachin Tendulkar, and one of his best friends is Abhishek Sharma.

> 'Patience is very important, especially in Test cricket.'
>
> — SHUBMAN GILL

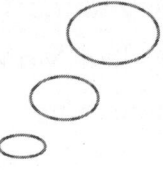

11
EPILOGUE

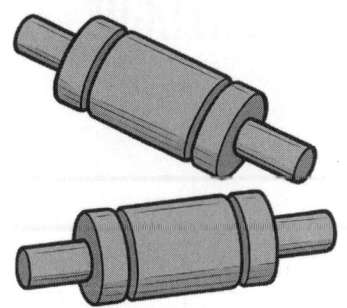

SHUBMAN GILL NAMED ICC PLAYER OF THE MONTH FOR JULY 2025

Gill became the first male player to win the Player of the Month award four times after a stupendous run in England saw him score 567 runs at an average of 94.50 in the three Tests played in July. His previous ICC Player of the Month awards were in January 2023, September 2023 and February 2025.

This isn't the first time Shubman is named ICC Player of the Month, a prestigious monthly recognition from the International Cricket

Council, but it feels more special to him than any previous version of the award. When asked about the fourth award, he says:

> It feels great to be named the ICC Player of the Month for July. This time it holds a lot more significance since it has come for my performances during my first Test series as captain. The Test series against England was a learning experience for me as captain and we had some outstanding performances from both sides, which I am sure players from both sides will remember for a long time.

The ICC's congratulatory post is polished, brief, flattering.

But this time, it feels different.

Maybe it's because it came after three hard-fought Tests in England, the kind of series that leaves you bruised in places you didn't know could ache. Or maybe it's because this time

he wasn't just playing in the series, he was leading it.

567 runs. Three Tests. An average of 94.5.

Staggering numbers, if you stop to think about it, although Shubman always thinks he's better off looking ahead to the next innings rather than resting on his laurels. Regardless, these numbers aren't the kind you process all at once. Beyond the numbers, it is the rhythm of it all.

The long hours at the crease. The conversations in the slips. The calls he had to make: when to declare, who to bowl, when to trust instinct over plan.

He receives news of the award in his hotel room, somewhere between packing and the long flight home. He reads the press release. Then the quote they've pulled from him – something about leadership and learning, and the memory of good cricket.

And it's all true.

But what he doesn't say, what doesn't make the quote, is how this version of the award carries something else. It's proof.

Proof that he can step into something larger than himself. That he can wear the weight of a team, a series, a legacy that blazes before him, bright, shining, beloved, and still stand tall.

Later, he folds the blazer he wore at the toss. Places it on top of his kit bag.

Four-time ICC Player of the Month. India's Test captain. And still, somehow, Shubman Gill feels like he's just getting started.

'If there's one thing I've learned from cricket, it's that life is full of surprises. My journey has been full of ups and downs, but through consistent hard work and discipline, I've managed to stay on course.'

— SHUBMAN GILL

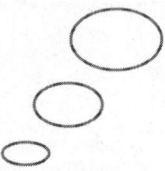

SHUBMAN GILL: THE FACT FILE

LET'S TALK MILESTONES

Shubman Gill holds the record for the 2nd most runs scored by a team captain in Test matches with 754 runs, and the most runs scored by an Indian team captain in Test cricket, even higher than the legendary Sunil Gavaskar. The only captain to have scored more runs than him is the Australian cricketer, Donald Bradman – also known as Don Bradman – who made 810 runs in 1936 against England in the famed Ashes series.

Shubman has also scored a century each in both innings of a Test match against England in Birmingham in 2025. He made 216 runs in the first innings, and 161 runs in the second. Interestingly, Shubman also had the bad luck of being dismissed for a duck – at 0 runs – in Chennai in 2024 in the first match of a Test match against Bangladesh. In the second innings, however, he went on to score 119 and held his wicket at the end of the match.

Shubman now holds the record for the fastest batter to make 2000 runs in the ODI format. He took only 38 matches to reach the milestone, four years after his ODI debut in 2019.

TEST
FORMAT

37
MATCHES

61.42
STRIKE RATE

69
INNINGS

9
CENTURIES

5
NOT OUTS

7
HALF-CENTURIES

2647
RUNS

43
SIXES

269
HIGHEST SCORE

295
FOURS

41.35
AVERAGE SCORE

28
CATCHES

ODI FORMAT

55 MATCHES	**99.56** STRIKE RATE
55 INNINGS	**8** CENTURIES
8 NOT OUTS	**15** HALF-CENTURIES
2775 RUNS	**59** SIXES
208 HIGHEST SCORE	**313** FOURS
59.04 AVERAGE SCORE	**37** CATCHES

T20I
FORMAT

28
MATCHES

141.28
STRIKE RATE

28
INNINGS

1
CENTURIES

3
NOT OUTS

15
HALF-CENTURIES

705
RUNS

24
SIXES

126*
HIGHEST SCORE

77
FOURS

28.2
AVERAGE SCORE

8
CATCHES

LIST A
FORMAT

110
MATCHES

94.39
STRIKE RATE

109
INNINGS

14
CENTURIES

14
NOT OUTS

26
HALF-CENTURIES

5039
RUNS

100
SIXES

208
HIGHEST SCORE

542
FOURS

53.04
AVERAGE SCORE

63
CATCHES

FIRST-CLASS

66
MATCHES

66.76
STRIKE RATE

117
INNINGS

18
CENTURIES

10
NOT OUTS

19
HALF-CENTURIES

5341
RUNS

80
SIXES

269
HIGHEST SCORE

622
FOURS

49.91
AVERAGE SCORE

47
CATCHES

FEATS

FASTEST TO 2000
RUNS - ODI

SECOND FASTEST
TO 1000 RUNS - ODI

SECOND MOST RUNS
IN A SERIES BY
A CAPTAIN   754

SECOND HIGHEST
CAREER BATTING   59.04
AVERAGE - ODI

SECOND MOST RUNS
IN A MATCH – TEST   430

SECOND MOST
HUNDREDS IN A   4
SERIES

OTHER BOOKS IN THE SERIES

You need unshakeable belief to be a champion, no matter where you come from. From growing up as a poor kid whose family couldn't afford his coaching to smashing world records, Rohit's journey has been full of never-give-up moments. Follow him through his school days, his ups and downs, the epic captaincy wins and, of course, the super-duper, totally amazing World Cup. Here's a warning: once you start reading this book, you may just not be able to stop.

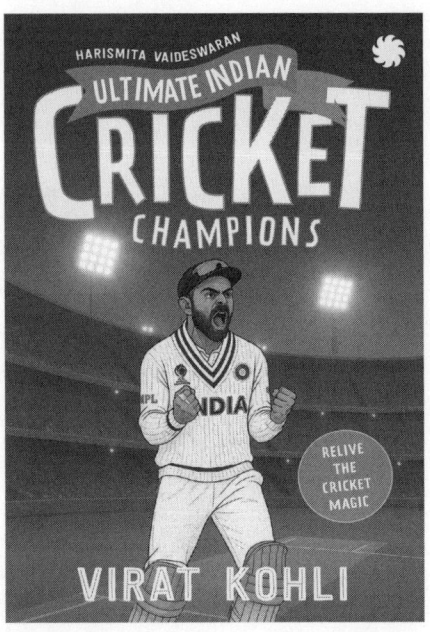

Virat Kohli was obsessed with being no. 1 right from the start. So laser-sharp was his focus that he continued to play cricket even after learning that his dad had died – he was only eighteen! In this action-packed, high-energy book, relive his greatest matches, his record-breaking plays and get inside the mind of a champ who turned challenges into victories, lifted cups and inspired millions. Here's a warning: once you start reading this book, you may just not be able to stop.